D1152956

Modern Times

The Daily Telegraph

Modern Times

ORION

Orion Books
A division of the Orion Publishing Group Ltd
Orion House
5 Upper St Martin's Lane
London
WC2H 9EA

This collected edition first published by
Orion Books Ltd in 2003

Copyright © The Daily Telegraph 2003

The right of Matthew Pritchett to be identified
as the author of this work has been asserted by him
in accordance with the Copyright, Designs
and Patents Act, 1988

A CIP catalogue record for this book
is available from the British Library

ISBN 0 75285 841 6

All rights reserved
No part of this publication may be reproduced,
stored in a retrieval system, or transmitted, in any form
or by any means, electronic, mechanical, photocopying,
recording or otherwise, without the prior permission in
writing of the publishers, nor be otherwise circulated in
any form of binding or cover other than that in which it is
published and without a similar condition including this
condition being imposed on the subsequent purchaser.

Printed and bound in Great Britain by
Clays Ltd, St Ives plc

FOREWORD

Thank you for buying the new hands-free *Modern Times* digital cartoon book. It's important that you charge the battery (recharger and leads supplied) for 24 hours *before* you start reading the book. There are details in your instruction manual on how to set up your microwave oven to text message the cartoons to your mobile phone. Or, if you want to read the book while driving, your satellite navigation system can now download the drawings and display them on your dashboard, while a friendly German voice reads out the captions in any one of 90 languages.

Next year we're launching the Virtual Reality Book. State of the art 3D goggles and glove sensors create the impression of really turning the pages.

Alternatively, you could just leave this book, along with all your other cartoon books, in the loo.

MATT

Modern Times

'If anyone here knows of any reason why these two people cannot move their stuff into a flat...'

'Our son is a bit of a hot headed
political activist – he voted in
the local elections'

'I know I agreed to be a
surrogate mother, but I've
decided I want to keep
20,000 of them'

'My business has taken over
this hospital and I'm afraid
I'm going to have to let you go'

'Nobody's given me any money,
but I've been shortlisted for
the Turner Prize'

'It's a rat race, you take
the test at seven, and you're
burned out at eight'

'I can't remember the exact
date of birth, but I know
petrol was £2.27'

'Let's just say we encourage
our employees to work
on Sundays'

'Smacking or non smacking?'

'And when the music stops...'

'He's been there since last weekend trying to put the clock back'

'He's the only one who can work
the video machine'

'The vicar's trying to
compete with the Sunday-
opening supermarkets'

'We've had an attractive trans-
fer offer for you from a school
lower down the league'

'Let's use the toaster for
now and we'll try nuclear
fusion again tomorrow'

'I can't help thinking that if I had been caned at school none of this would have happened'

'Eureka! I've cloned
mint sauce'

'How ironic, we've just had a
near miss with the plane my
luggage is on'

'Have you met my husband?
He's a weather forecaster'

'We've put nicotine patches
over the names of the
tobacco companies'

'Is it for casseroling
or transplanting'

'I see you haven't quite
got the hang of kilos yet'

'Let's play doctors and
nurses – I'll report you
for incompetence'

'At least we know you're
not taking performance-
enhancing drugs'

'Hello, darling, I've done
most of the shopping, but did
you say washing powder was
cheaper in Spain or France'

'I just want to say thank you'

'In the old days we'd just get
a clip round the ear'

'Your university days are some of the happiest of my life'

'Hurry up, come and eat your
supper before the government
decides to ban it'

'He's feeding well but I'm
worried that he still hasn't
done anything about
his pension'

'I'm £10,000 in debt after being at the university of life'

'I note that your essay is
overdue. You have been
charged £25 for this letter'

'I've either just done our
weekly shop at Tesco,
or I've adopted twins'

'WAIT!...I can make
RoboDog wave goodbye'

'I've merged with
an internet company'

'Are you friends of the bride or
of the groom's first wife?'

'It says computer hackers have
been reading our e-mail messages'

'I wanted to concentrate
on my career, so I've
had my eggs poached'

'It's much harder to fail
exams than it was in your day'

'We can use Consignia or a
private mail company'

'Ladies and gentlemen,
we're very close to creating
the ideal human being'

'Is that your new aftershave
or has there been a
chemical warfare attack?'

'Hello, my cat is stuck up a
tree, could someone clone
another one for me?'

'The Fire Service, please'

'Try throwing money at me'

'Sarge, I think these scales
are in pounds and ounces'